GONGO DODAN

Gustave Morin

D1522246

NEW STAR BOOKS | VANCOUVER | 2022

NEW STAR BOOKS LTD

No. 107–3477 Commercial St, Vancouver, BC V5N 4E8 CANADA

1574 Gulf Road, No. 1517 Point Roberts, WA 98281 USA

newstarbooks.com · info@newstarbooks.com

The publisher acknowledges the financial support of the Canada Council for the Arts, the British Columbia Arts Council, and the Government of Canada.

Supported by the Province of British Columbia

Cataloguing information for this book is available from Library and Archives Canada, www.collectionscanada.gc.ca.

ISBN: 9781554201860

Cover art: Door Stop, by Gustave Morin (2016)

Cover design by Oliver McPartlin

Typeset by New Star Books

Printed and bound in Canada by Imprimerie Gauvin, Gatineau, QC

First printing April 2022

to the memory of
Steve Schneider (1952 : 2021)
with love

table of contents

.//.

If a book is worth reading, it's worth buying.
                                        – Ruskin

Words are the only things that last forever.
                                        – Hazlitt

To write prose, one must have something to say;
but who has nothing to say can still make verses
and rhymes, where one word suggests the other,
and at last something comes out which in fact is
nothing but looks as if it were something.
                                        – Goethe

ez
pz

she plants flowers to have some
thing to fall back in
to.

bread & flame & noise
(for the candy butcher

... zip oozing out: POW ! steal
a bit: AND HOW ! you seldom if
we smite your name; you never
some battleship burnt. HEY LOOK:
the plot sickens — give it
a little loop / knock-knock
jam that king mob cries crash
AND HOW ! its rumoured that
I'm tick / boom. an old taste
bent massive but not broken
as surely as you're sitting there.

mongrel we say zoom through
zounds; tempest when tent
a foul mouth / beep beep
that crime questions head
off with the head only look
in our minds; event ways to
screaming / spare a little
rough, broken chairs with
any light. face the line
at nobody so & so to take
the wall to blast you good
AND HOW are you going?
nova?

go it a
lone wolf
wit / pith
with

the wolf(e) life

...knew his life was a little
image of man/s whole squish —
and that only seemed to him
all the more all and ever-
lasting; tiny spurts of flame
dying with defiance over
shoots & shouts of denial.
all our grandeur, pulse
of heart & epic glory
comes from engulfing
night...

...and of this flame, it
there & then came to him
that he would be extinguished.
life upon the earth — its
darkness was immense. life
like a time we knew we would
blaze out briefly by these
lips, & that the darkness
would ring with the last
tragic dignity — our heroes
into the maw of all the
brevity and small...

warped small dogs driving
zippy cars
woof !

the tape cars on the televisions in our homes have televisions
in those cars broadcasting
bullets as they rip
down the roads roaring
from scene to screen
to scream shooting blue
light into all our
brains idling . . .

they have bullets from idle blue shots rearing broadcasts
into homes like holes
in the roads the brains
scream at cars ripping
televisions from the scene
through the screen as obscenely
idle blue light flickers
at flailing holes . . .

the roaring on television at holes screen bullets
into brains from the blue
light broadcasts rippling
the flicker obscene; holes
like homes roaring idle
blue light flailing from shots
as the bullets rip-rearing
broadcasts shoot home . . .

yon

seek a peak:
reed / enter
,almost big

     *

work an ice egg — the ear
wet, the years
run

     *

let air despise
ode errors / youth
first to example

     *

to hear close
go err beyond

     *

the form / it
of our image
ships dilligent inks

     *

every good horror
& ape gift
is no tower

the void inn
tasted / & guests
dine time among

*

d,e,s,o,l,a,t,e
for live intent
in the soot

*

let era do to troubled
ropes, dirt-fast
,afraid

*

have stone sores —
let offence diet

*

half this say
pled a right leper (& dreamed
t.n.t. with a many them

*

because die
this armed meaning
per. . .

th	ef	or	me
xp	re	ss	es
wh	at	th	ec
on	te	nt	is
me	an	tt	od
is	gu	is	e.

as the walls close in the pinch is felt by those not turning the screws
as the walls close in the pinch is felt by those not turning the scre
ws as the walls close in the pinch is felt by those not turning the
screws as the walls close in the pinch is felt by those not turni
ng the screws as the walls close in the pinch is felt by those
not turning the screws as the walls close in the pinch is fe
lt by those not turning the screws as the walls close in t
he pinch is felt by those not turning the screws as the
walls close in the pinch is felt by those not turning
the screws as the walls close in the pinch is felt
by those not turning the screws as the walls clo
se in the pinch is felt by those not turning t
he screws as the walls close in the pinch is
felt by those not turning the screws as th
e walls close in the pinch is felt by th
ose not turning the screws as the wall
s close in the pinch is felt by thos
e not turning the screws as the wa
lls close in the pinch is felt b
y those not turning the screws
as the walls close in the pi
nch is felt by those not t
urning the screws as the
walls close in the pin
ch is felt by those
not turning the s
crews as the wa
lls close in
the pinch
is felt
by th
ose
not
t
u
r
n
i
n
g
t
h
e
s
c
r
e
w
s
.

open the news
— paper & the f —
lies pour out

putting the brave face on the expensive junkyard

... when the wolves lick the kings, the kings turn
into wolves; wolves built a smidge above minimum —
and when they say image you better believe they mean
money: where we had companies we now have company.

as ever, agency is conferred, not taken; the informed
are all uniformed; what goes over the top tends to scrape
from the bottom, i.e., government is private office.
there is no line to cut on between the rotten meat &

the part of the meat not rotten — the only things moving
through these ruins are flies. whatever deepens also dim-
inishes, & vice versa: whether upheld or broken, the law
exists for scumbags — hatchetjobs for hatchetmen armed

with hatchets & well-worn copies of hamlet. first we complain
and then we comply, but our bloodthirst is wasted on cretins.

brussels sprouts

. . . .

muscle cars

ex-motorcity

no one has ever written the land into a line —
& now there's no reason to; too, a century entered
the plants to carve out the cars up from their
moulds a hunted bounty belaboured the earth;
its outgrowth tiring haunted small cities strung
along one long roped-in garland of crumbs fronting
a marshland of crimes swept under the smug pulled
out & spun spinning out reinvented wheels broken
on the wheel of fortune cookie crumbled as wheels
within wheels once upon a time rolled off a line
underwritten by thin pay every day leeched out
by these plants advanced a horde of boarded-up
rubble in rusty neglect; its transit rewards our
puny expressway while most roads turn trail.

code is a cheat away from the green light
for & after randall brock (1943 : 2012)

harsh light
alive, a grip
of mouth
loose in a yawn
before a television .

you are the
blessing of
a young
and restless
tornado warning
label .

a quick twist
singing the blue
murder about
a nerve
chewing hate .

releasing the red
breakdown of
a greedy
ear swallowing
life-like
lives, glistening .

rustic stitch
of a dirty knife
trick below
the ocean, a fiction
of copper or
cardboard .

warm soft belly
of an icicle
melting the shiver
of a captured
lunatic fringe
festival .

water of a full
pit clearing
away the stones
of an angle
in your skeleton
closet .

pink earth
of a noise
sewing the copper
or cardboard of
a slate above or
below, same dif .

once nonce

texcie mopie plextal sink

tuno tal tuno

brak fisbis

texcie sink

zimzum

—

zimzum sink texcie

tuno tal tuno

mopie brak plextal fisbis

texcie sink

zimzum

won't abide

won't abide
furry grey
precincts of area where
vagaries experienced
by the open mouth
bargain for a fist
mailed with stamps
or a kiss yellowing under
bland concern showing
the technique of vacuum
neatly subtracted from
the enclosed fur invention –
& like all knuckle-dragging
grapplings with vulgar
reality in actuality
won't due to describe
a hybrid swirl fit to be
tied down to a place or
to a time before
a vertical access
up along the spine
plummeted most
into poverty of incident
where none of our sounds
ever dried up

les scribblistes

gasp the world that speaks the word
pains the word & scatters the world
the world: the word word 'invariting'
forgetting loss of memory ...

falling from the outside / an alien
form, the human body / writing ...
(i forgot: <u>i had too blood</u>, wordless)

5 human senses) wood (5 human
senses (the wound, there was none.)
years went by noise, sleep, darkness

muddy streets, the creak afraid —
mistakes scribe the bones stranded
in the centuries ... hallucinating

words in air, severed heads kissing
(blood, i thought) clear as pain,
glass to break / bones the colour blue

edge sinking, light hurt a rooftop:
an image, a mountain forgotten
the trance exhausted ...

<u>to be human at last</u> / "it taste so good"
a storm coming ... dark continuing ...
the body will scream in simple sunshine .

a certain man who went bad wrote
the story twisting centuries,
crappy endings abandoned

wandering looped twilight . ornament
(a shiver) in worthless toil bent .
shadows story years no one noticed
darkness cut off at the neck ...

market greed splinters what tables scavenge
(broken words become writing torn)
dogs flicker past baubles fast .

power in kind, in coin: things
pain fails to speak / reenact
an embrace, asleep, grey dawn curts .

song, terrified: bang a jar, messy
flaws that split silence . leprosy
the text; waive what is written ...

but that stain really happened —
"it is finished", lantern dark &
smiles being alive being alive so

erase all signatures, small bones smashed
tell the stories / disappear along muddy
streets, dusty paths, words unspoken

the pork
chop on
the porch
hops

see thing
seething / talking
heads on
sticks making
nice turvey
topsey / bloody
knows chews
life; say mould
same old carry on
carrion / small
canvas afraid at
the edges kiss
kiss jump cuts
bang bang cuts
jump ship
shape shifter
as yawp-o-maw
blurts eons
o'peons
turmoil of data:
...bother of spot
...grey it paint
...hand to month

tryst

...of my me it is not in I
: but the you that she had on
was for he too, with a have
and a has not .

she too was the it of my in,
not had for that...but he
has an 'is me' and I have
AT on with you .

but it is not <u>she</u>, on at my he
for the me that i have ? (and
was a has of you in with
the had too ?)

and in you (at that) she too
was a have-me-not for my he-has.
...but of the 'it is'
i have on with..?

not a but has he have for me;
is with you I had my in too.
that was the it of at —
AND on she...

and on, he of is has a she for the it
that was with you...but me too,
i have not had at
my in...

I have no but with the has that
he had — and my, she is for me:
not in of at it too
was a you.

he was had but for that; I have
the has, not an at. in my me —
of you — she is on
and with it too.

for fk

half-maxims for sloppy cannibals

1. too many books loyal to sloth.

2. its always carcass before the yawn.

3. give them a cinch and they take a while.

4. pie before tea except after 3.

5. factions clique prouder than turds.

6. one good burn deserves a brother.

7. it doesn't matter how you spin the clues its how you lay the frame.

8. where there's a kill there's a fray.

9. don't book a seahorse in the south.

10. a brain is only as wrong as its meekest think.

11. a fool and his money are still retarded.

12. that's like the cop calling the meadow crap.

13. every wooden ploy deserves sludge.

14. all baths of gory plead to the brave.

15. affluence makes the smart flow yonder.

16. man does not spiv by head alone.

17. a penny paved is a penny spurned.

18. all the spit that is curled is tossed on he who has won.

19. you lonely heap what few give delay.

20. when the caveat's made of clay the paradise will decay.

21. you can't beat your steak and stab it too.

22. keep your trends close and your centipedes closer.

23. a bounce of attention will birth a round of blur.

24. sailing to a fair is repairing to jail.

25. you can't beseech a demagogue to screw politics.

26. people who give in crass blouses shouldn't stow moans.

27. put your funny where your south is.

28. if wigs could cry they would have stings.

29. with hens like scat who feeds the den of thieves?

30. if squishes were sources twigs would abide.

31. chair the flawed and toil the wild.

32. she that stuns may breed.

33. a botched ought never spoils.

34. what's food for the noose is food for the banter.

35. two thongs don't make a sight.

36. you can breed a force to slaughter but you can't make it think

37. you only squirt the ones you glove

38. trite makes blight.

39. out of the trying span and into the quagmire

40. no one collides for brie.

41. every frown taunts to grey omellette.

42. the code to jezebel is depraved by misunderstood conventions.

43. each man thrills the thing he rubs.

44. absurd in demand will berth spew in the push.

45. a grapple astray weeps the stalker at bay.

46. many blands make bright murk.

47. a bitch in crime is a waste of time.

48. the surley word gets the squirm.

49. know and already grins the face.

50. the ring of snooty is a ploy for never.

51. all that fritters is not sold.

52. too many books foil the sloth

woodpecker
working the telephone
pole

wood bee

...call it the edge is serrated
by proxy; but brief it gruesome
then cut it in half, all leave taken
fleeting on feats of endurance vile
like a sixth toe towing a thirteenth
month, or a mothballed film fogged fast
when inked by jet & rejecting an object
in terms the reverse of an aesthetic split
second words in the sky scraped sight reading
into where tooth clawed way out of the cavern
a tavern neither along for the ride nor part of any
road worthy cause & effect, just a pack of rainier lives
starring nothing more than contempt for bodies dissolving
under the heft of a sparkle drubbing the painted corner where
any fell sky scraping the bottom always keeps x. meanwhile our
profound sublime turns to slime for solace knowing entropy to be
the only real profundity & every world view an incomplete foot on
neck or in mouth punching weigh above weight lifting the bronze to
settle for pewter all the while weaving tumult into dreams by making
do without dorsal fins breaking open the water & finishing off the last
of the 99 bottles of beer on the wall & calling it the edge, serrated by
proxy...

givens are often
the first to go
& gone should be
a familiar
similar
as a betrayal
we are driven
over to wanting
less, less
through the condition
of rubbing elbows
with the rank
& file under outrage
or apathy, but more
through excess of
obstacle conditioned
be the rote
vanishings have writ

CA$H

though the sleep would grind to glass
half awake slivers melt the heart in
to vain pieces when of a suddenly
glass could see to back of the eyes
closed & then seizing those insides
for the plain & unable to go through
the ceiling would off sleep on the bed

then the bed wakes up to half explode
strange slates pumped through eyes
while brain floats a stomach sold
to see being grow on time & expand
a would-be nightmare in the bloodstream
come again to roof the glass with care/
of infinity closed out & turned over

hash oil
on gramma's X-
muss card

: f l u r r i e s

a pint of beer
fits a gravy
boat perfectly

beat lake

silly my bold survival rate without swan language:
up the cover to happy poet pet clouds lining all

other ranches like dark alien corn conjuring vows
fed on elation which smash sad districts into the

beautiful restless survival of the rest. end time
survives too while flaws flow to a fin out a lake,

and being left-handed, nests soggy into the pimp
swamp to watch ice when its waters left a lake

leftover like decay when it flowed at turning
knowing flaws from summer fled. such will daily

table sad beat of dusky way as youth moves when
creeping in touch, or when kicked upstairs near

beat lake to speak such sun flaws as chilled to
be bereft of the gift that never was, as it were.

the limerick police held a clambake
fine folk attended wishing to partake
of obscene things done with bugs,
unlubed fistings, minors on drugs
while K/9 feces laced the sponge cake.

big ticket

all rains in now, but when in metal
made a main one then unstable, the others
remained iron people — no cure for their
tower, no storm for that stage — but then
their antlers of glass kind of wilted the
ages; for to be able thoughts to be steel
high the bone up here grubs time out that
far day when concrete summer sun of root
shouts brought luck willing the way time
leaps around core rusts on pierced bronze
while people in nothing off cities splinter
a mountain over a poem made of plaster: a
door so stained wins the dump holiday in
the world's furthest threaded up mound .

**let sleeping lies
dog eat dog
biscuit**

the cant joint

in lazy light, would-be power now kicks
fine; sticks to the head in it nix wow
like zaps. grow those pay sticks & you'll
total reality, but not now nor yet so don't
cry over what would from a hospital. jumping
them up, fight like your tax grave took major
roads on maps thereby letting zips force the
most wise to sell at home. also, cease all
quacking skull hammer music withal fewer
than the foul suffering bright dog fever
ever will: poor girl, not a night to juke
box, or to provide a will to bring quirk
to be as before, casing the cant joint to
see who had the last jig out & aboutface

monster roar horn

toot! toot-toot-toot!   toot!   toot-toot-toot!

RROOOAAAARRR!!!!   RROOOAAAARRR!!!!

...crunchcrunchcrunchcrunchcrunch...

Ahhhhh...   crunchcrunchcrunch   Ahhhhh...

RROOOAAAARRR!!!!   RROOOAAAARRR!!!!

Ahhhhh...   Ahhhhh...   Ahhhhh...

...crunchcrunchcrunchcrunchcrunch...

toot!   toot-toot-toot-!   toot!   toot-toot-toot!

SCKRRREEEECCHHH !   SCKRRREEEECCHHH !

Ahhhhh...   Ahhhhh...   Ahhhhhhhhhhhhhh !

...crunchcrunchcrunchcrunchcrunch...

toot!   toot-toot-toot!

SCKRRREEEECCHHH !

Ahhhhhhhhhhhhhhhhhhhhhhhhhhhhhh !

the rent lions

knowing sabres rattle for cash to register a ditch
stands at the very end of the strait for war is just

another kiosk tasking a people cornered and was never
thunder or overmuch of anything else since doom secretes

rex middleman rightwing pay per view bloopers provided
spec wars spent street fortunes abroad in lieu of an e-

conomy while our domestic face caved in and mouths
ajar most willingly gasped blood or grasped straws

for slurping rituals while groping their tribal score —
a trophy bright circus light on ancient sands beside

a burnt fountain as the news sad to say and the news
black and white with dread all over reported what

those low rent lions devoted their entire lives to:
carefully guarding secrets beneath their own pride

**popcorn
burst of feathers
at 110 kph**

scratch that tundra

the mean universe hit light to break sky
then lost its low tower down olde route
never when it glimpsed that hollow waste
might enlist rust rivers on the banks of
despair once & all too late dividing hate
airs into shadows from eyes heaving woes
that hurt all who scraped some silence
overheard & in its final tune knew from
broken cult worldwide that these waves
would regard the oars weak when up no
mountain where certain scars sent to sour
skill in on the fat that may soon teach
someone for the slant the ache that is in
the ink from all the stolen & swollen books

for the canadian arthur cravan

taking the
pulse
of a thief
eating
a knuckle
sandwich
in a passing
neon
canoe

dues

may a page return gain for fearful keepers
of the scale when mush that is squared away
claims a worth nearly vouched for yet denying
proof that the power of its nearly reality
could be conveyed by accomplices who did
most of the heavy lifting up a few untoward
deeds completely out of talent or of agency

rewards established bring in such disregard
that the writer (unlike so many of shallow re-
search i.e. alone of surplus) explored for that
other sake — the thing inked in as a solid
living knowledge so intense such energy made
the hope craven until courage would pledge
much idly put need of action back into play

47

alone in our bodies   life
sweeps in and decades
the tissue

this awesome dust

standstill seen by how wild west stops all tree time:
like sheep in cold folds, dull heads in skulls cornered
go far right on our tired dead star. most places seige
adjusted ghost incomes, so pain blue nocturnes in the
trees must instead undersell their fancy. furious when
down time opened out to lies lowly wishing cut flowers
would write on cancelled ice, this awesome dust whirls
suddenly seeing thin white light shatter the dark plume
crawling down from the head when finished fielding for-
ever. rain leaning over sure stayed pretty odd by day,
but by night slowly it creeps up to danger as the torn
failure leaks a solid wrath that will reign dead in
the water should these sails fold up to a sky whose
vast songbag will always be as mute as a riot . . .

. . . for jwcurry. . .

49

~~Leave well enough alone~~

~~Enough Leave well alone~~

~~Well leave enough alone~~

~~Alone well leave enough~~

~~Well leave alone enough~~

~~Enough alone leave well~~

~~Leave enough well alone~~

~~Alone well enough leave~~

~~Well alone leave enough~~

Leave well enough alone

witness appeal

depth failed school knowing the sage rides
all material greedily as things that imperil
constrain to see the culture dictate force
fed on world luxury goods going horribly
larger nowadays when industry states this
thin patch is not just misery placed into
a house held come to ring in the new fear

going to work up cruel land full debt free
to displace order around the kit of sleepless
nights ripping the lost free year from the
last free future shocking social confusion
seen listing our work weak award won aesthetic
fists so oft on the lips increasing faux wealth
as new strains talk shops into part time despairs

dogs are shiny?

eggs i hear

DNA Inc.

no longer young yet perched darkly to recall
strains of small moment when the token crawl
from a place the slime alighted on from beyond
the stink of learning to curve this soiled hand
had bozo spanking without spark or willful flair
while oozing bland galleries had been flung open
to siphon off their trivial and tedious shares

unknown subjects in charge to hazard repair
catch breath fled from the bends below woes
which no sooner scold the unfolding chaos
run aground when heavy blade formation in
disguise but lately issued without slight
or provocation climbed like vine over little
clay strips hung up in the ruins of ether

**i dropped a piece of tape & it landed sticky-side
up!**

hotel atlantis

when triumph aligns with a page amid all these
scary eyes closed against the grain the funniest

wolf at the dog park will draw a tension to the
second best museum scraps milking double doses

of kinder property knives clamouring to be stuck
to the squirming people as the next great big

thing becomes a living awfully beyond our means
as against those dreams born when america strolled

in to this life and its swollen culture collapsed
into 24 hour news which shattered precious moments

allowing some nameless punk wearing a greasy sand-
wich board to exploit a forsaken cut of meat at

the second annual junk consciousness awards ceremony
held in the elegant basement of the hotel atlantis

— for & after DfB

none de la less

he thought
the world of thought.

the world he thought
the world of
thought not.

not that the world
he thought the world of
thought not

just that
he thought the world
of thought

yet the world
he thought the world of
thought not.

motley oxen

after plundering the ancient sea to redeem
this grave and dour albeit exalted sunspot
the day carried shrift short when geometry
blotted out poesy despite labouring in dark
labyrinths and following orders to not taste
the wail should the perfect beasts refuse
all dreams to send wisdom packing for good

and/or bad company as the worship of signs
expressed in fountains sustain this sting-
song and dance the whole ache in witless
style if stories tapping the highest vein
hope to hear told the brave ink cast away
by fools cold novel language when these
oxen of human life play agony for sport

the gusto was robust

& then we turned to

dust

generations

the entire history of humanity works
through a blazing up of water just as
it works through the wound of the word
blood drawn back to matter should we
move our last in an epidemic hardly
noticed by the cosmos at a time when
the pace of history faster than ideas

we breathe in air a flood more cruel
than nature or the times when we are
annihilated bloodsheed attains its end
by the sight of our arms in the fire
since disturbance cannot crush conflict
we remain swallowed up when our passed
over dead bodies calmly obey all laws

．blague konst ．churl plurch ．

dag nab   drek daubs

,

outered

wharves

should quagmires be burnt to pavement
feats won't harden to rock lest yarns

explore terrifying cliffs of mud where
by a detested cold sun whose outer zones

could amend a warm shiver and so recover
compressed passage darkly or brightly spun

against that stream of time scaled to secrete
the gathering ranks composed of the rankled

laying planks over waters which duly signal
for the few fit navigators to continue in

pushing off from such extremes of place when
ever bold quays climb aloft long before our

trim race sought out and bought in toward
this cramped and indiscreet oblivion claw

with my eyes closed
the view is incredible

five and dime

darkness lifted off a noose of common clay
letting those good old days go where minutes
to go still tick tock towed a line through
streets of crumbling shade only to call time
out when those same frayed ropes were well
within striking distance of just about any
shadow of a pouch from whence all falling
stars knew to knock twice before taking it
outside to get behind a beast crying gently
hurt by these savage bare knuckle and dime
schemes living longer and dying slower than
five hole fingers holding more words about
the neck while dirty dancing to swaying from
almost extinct swing low sweet hanging vines

valhalla for teens

should joy not meant for strife rerun aground
while forked tongues for swords fall from lips
seeing clear the careless way thought or might
overcomes the meaning of postmodern changelings
struck dumb by future deserts never quite secure
enough to reroute all dull heart to heartless
desire from feckless evenings into afternoons

playing the whole world shallow for some new
slight or rage to shine off the party or page
to turn a life sentence of constancy and rule
into words banishing wisdom to ring grit true
before getting another today darkly grown with
out benefit of youth marked lost when profound
wanting from limb and life force fully fledged

the captain hates the sea

staring down chaos from the littlest height
below the rust belt to rue the spot on raw
the grandest stand alone sits pretty ugly
by dark stains hewn shapeless while further
afield antiquity arose from the same sticks
as if each age repaid its own debt of breath
with depth of threat as another ghostly sky
swore out another complaint against runny
rivers falling behind this wrecked shipment
down the drain while the joy of golden light
years to come in some glorious hole whereby
all faint visions so promised to be will be
wined and dined amid swizzle styx and stones
breaking open skull and crossbones for free

for david baptiste chirot (1953 : 2021)

all mod cons

even though the world keeps changing buildings
fires thirst bested a greater burn fading from
the concealed source sent with equal resolve to
those slams growing bigger when the sing song
said that removal of death produced passionate
drives so instead of obeying machine parts en-
chanted to be free of the turmoil suddenly all
flower and book messengers to life belong only
if hardcore steel guts fled the pride of grime
taken on as trifles imagine a darkness neither
knowledge based nor mindful of an exalted wrath
building yet more unusable space to make bold
its dim din of nil while meanwhile over landfill
all perfect things bad music limitlessly marvels

origin grinder

as the great sun toiling in the fields slowly
moves in on beasts whose thoughtless breath
may touch the taller grasses long before any
tape delay jars the bright eyed creatures from
beyond the wilder space where downcast heads
used to calmer plights might still ply letters
for polite excuses after the oblong grime spree

today mostly bids farewell to mark the fading
light fast with fading dyes aimed at straining
bright slights snuck out the cave and down a few
memory lanes as bags of watery salt muster to
live briefly while so sweetly the fly by night
life condemns the grey swamp for sudden pain as
dead of winter answers to all and hungry sundry

these immortal recoils

     i)

without wanting to be called names in the next
street where all the fairest pleasures of youth
are glossed over when abortion counsels eternity
by screaming down an emptiness laughed at with
endless fire of pain should dreams gather darkness
enough for idle fears wearing robes of inevitable
error to bring happiness to thousands of decades
whereby any beautiful concern for the art continues
to dread the worst of its unkindly justice so that
this cloudy life may also entertain the best cure
for returning to the fear of death by starving
out the mind full of all other jilted passages
growing narrower only to become hopelessly uniform
by dressing down every awe that had carried the day

ii)

then wisdoms slain hollow by overmuch council
infiltrates this going wrongheaded mock-tragic
hostage situation before scaring up an ambush
whacked checkered future into pulling out all
the shrill whistle stop signs of life fading to
black markets founded on the blankest realities
wandering blindfolded through yet another sterile
monoculture before tormented passions advancing
without passion vex grey daydreams into serving
notice that no possibility of rest can hope to
outsmart harm's sway ever since the furthest
breach from lowest hanging fruit to sawed off
lost labours loved a weary world that put paid to
mystery by deforming whatever still held delight

d   o   T

o   .

T   o   d

II.

Kudos to the custodians of the following splendid venues where some of these poems first appeared: Carousel, Ditch, fhole, The Lost and Found Times, Maple Spits, Van, and Where's The Little Dutch Boy? in NYC.

Also: Les Scribblistes was first published as a Produce Press chapbook in 2008; a selection of the Half-Maxims appeared anonymously in the Pocket Cannon anthology published anonymously in 2003; Dot was privately printed for Artscene in Windsor in 2002, to later reappear as Curv'd H&z # 467 as card # 105 in 2008; Easy Peasey first appeared in different form in The Big Tomato, published as Xerolage # 68 by Xexoxial of Wisconsin in 2018; as the walls… appeared in Just Like Cream But Worst issue 2 (Hordes of Drivel) published in Toronto in 2021.

Kudos to Steve McCaffery for penning the blurb that just wouldn't quit.

Kudos to Oona Mosna for performing her part in the first incarnation of Gongo Dodan back in 2001 & 2002 (Bug Death at Milk and Skinny Monday at the AGW).

Kudos to Patricia Fell and to Trevor Malcolm of the Pelee Island Stone and Sky Music and Art series for the art hut residencies in 2020 and in 2022.

Kudos to Jennifer Kimmerly of Standard Printing Inc. for the letterpress typesetting on both Easy Peasey and Dot.

Kudos to Rolf Maurer, Melissa Swann and to Vlad Cristache at New Star Books.

Kudos also due Hart Broudy, Bill Bissett, Michael E. Casteels, Brian Dedora, Marshall Hryciuk & Karen Sohne and to Michael Mann in Minnesota.

Kudos to Andrea Slavik and to Christine Burchnall for going to bat for Chthonic Youth at Artcite Inc. in Windsor in 2016.

Kudos to Viki, Kudos to Myriam, Kudos to Elizabeth, Kudos to Simone and Kudos to Nana Lori & Poppa Paul. XOXOXO!

Saving the best for last, Kudos to my awesome gals, the wonderful MS. Jenny K. & the amazing MS. Nova Faxon. XOXOXO!